MEZZO-SOPRANO

The First Book of Broadway S

Compiled

CW00421024

ISBN 0-634-02282-2

HAL•LEONARD®
CORPORATION
7777 W. Bluemound Rd. P.O. Box 13819 Milwaukee, WI 53213

Preface

When a beginning student of voice is ready for song literature, it is very important that some musical theatre material be included in the lesson repertoire. (This comment applies to American, Canadian, British, or other native English-speaking students.) Show tunes are a unique American and British contribution to the music world. Many of them are very useful for developing a smooth vocal line in an idiom that speaks to teenagers and new adult students. Not only is the music very melodic, the fact that the words are in a student's native language is an enormous advantage. *The First Book of Broadway Solos* attempts to address a traditional, classical voice teacher's sensibilities and needs in teaching basic techniques of singing.

The frustrations that I have experienced as a teacher are: (1) the vocal selection books from individual shows have, at most, two or three suitable songs for a particular voice; (2) the many piano/vocal show tune collections available have only several songs in good vocal study keys (mezzo-soprano being the exception); (3) the editions of songs taken from the actual vocal scores found in excellent publications such as *The Singer's Musical Theatre Anthology* are, in many cases, unsuitable for the beginning student because they are too long, too involved, and often in difficult keys for the novice singer.

The songs selected for *The First Book of Broadway Solos* were chosen for use by beginning voice students to assist in developing a solid vocal technique during the first several months or years of lessons. In most cases, the original voice category is preserved, although at times I chose, for musical and vocal reasons, to use a song originally sung by a baritone or tenor, for instance, in the mezzo-soprano collection (of course, taking into account the suitability of the text). Many keys have been altered to accommodate the ranges of the majority of teenagers and beginning adult students using these books. For those persons coming from a theatre point of view, it should be noted that these books are not designed for the belting style of singing. Specifically, mezzo-soprano is classically defined in this series (rather than the definition of this voice type by the theatre world as a belter). That is not to say that a more theatrical style of singing is not important or needed in other contexts. For the purposes of vocal instruction, classically based, lyric singing is the aim of this series.

Because many of the standard show tunes tend to be too low for the developing soprano voice, the majority of the keys in that volume have been raised. Most of the songs focus on a modest range comfortable for beginning singers, although several songs will showcase those students who are developing a higher vocal range. Many of the original keys, as published in the vocal selections of a show, were retained for the mezzo-soprano volume. More than half of the keys in the tenor collection have been raised to meet the vocal needs of the higher male voice. In most cases, the ranges in the baritone/bass volume have been lowered because the typical beginning baritone or bass struggles with the upper range tessitura and occasional high notes. A few of the songs were transposed down for the true bass range.

All the books include a few vocally challenging pieces, as well as a few more unfamiliar and unique entries. Overall, the songs in these four volumes include a wide variety of classics representative of the last seventy-five years of Broadway shows.

It is my hope that the studio voice teacher or the high school choral director will find this series a valuable resource, providing students with literature that is teachable, fun, and is an excellent introduction to the unique art form of musical theatre.

The First Book of Broadway Solos

Compiled by Joan Frey Boytim

AS LONG AS HE NEEDS ME

OLIVER!

Words and Music by
LIONEL BART

2
Cmaj7 C7 F G7 C
Me. If you are lone - ly then you will know When some - one
Am D9 Dm7 Fm G7 Cmaj7 G11 G13-9
needs you you love them so. I won't be - tray his
Cmaj7 A7-9 Dm7
trust, Tho' peo - ple say I must. I've got to
A7-9 Am7 D9 Dm7 Fm G7 C
stay true, just As Long As He Needs Me.
f

BALI HA'I

SOUTH PACIFIC

Lyrics by OSCAR HAMMERSTEIN II
Music by RICHARD RODGERS

Fm7
Bb
Bb7
One where they know they would like to be.
Ba - li
rit.
8vb
Refrain (slowly)
Ebdim
Eb
Ebdim
Eb
Ha'i may call you an - y night, An - y day. In your
p-mf
D
Cb7
Eb
Cb7
Bb7
Eb
heart you'll hear it call you: "Come a - way, Come a - way." Ba - li
Ebdim
Eb
Ebdim
Eb
Ha'i will whis - per On the wind of the sea: "Here am

D Cb7 Eb Cb7 Bb7 E
I, ___ Your spe-cial is - land! Come to me, come to me!" Your
Ab Ab+
own spe - cial hopes, Your own spe - cial dreams
mf
Fm Abm Bb7
Bloom on the hill - side And shine in the streams. If you
mp
Ebdim Eb Ebdim Eb
try, You'll find me Where the sky Meets the sea. "Here am

D
Cb7 Eb
Cb7
Bb7
I, Your spe - cial is - land! Come to me, Come to
Eb7
Ab
Bb9
1
Eb6
me!" Ba - li Ha'i, Ba - li Ha'i, Ba - li Ha'i!
cresc.
mf
Ddim
Cm
Ddim
Some day you'll see me, Float - ing in the
mp
Cm
Fdim
sun - shine, My head stick - ing out From a low - fly - ing

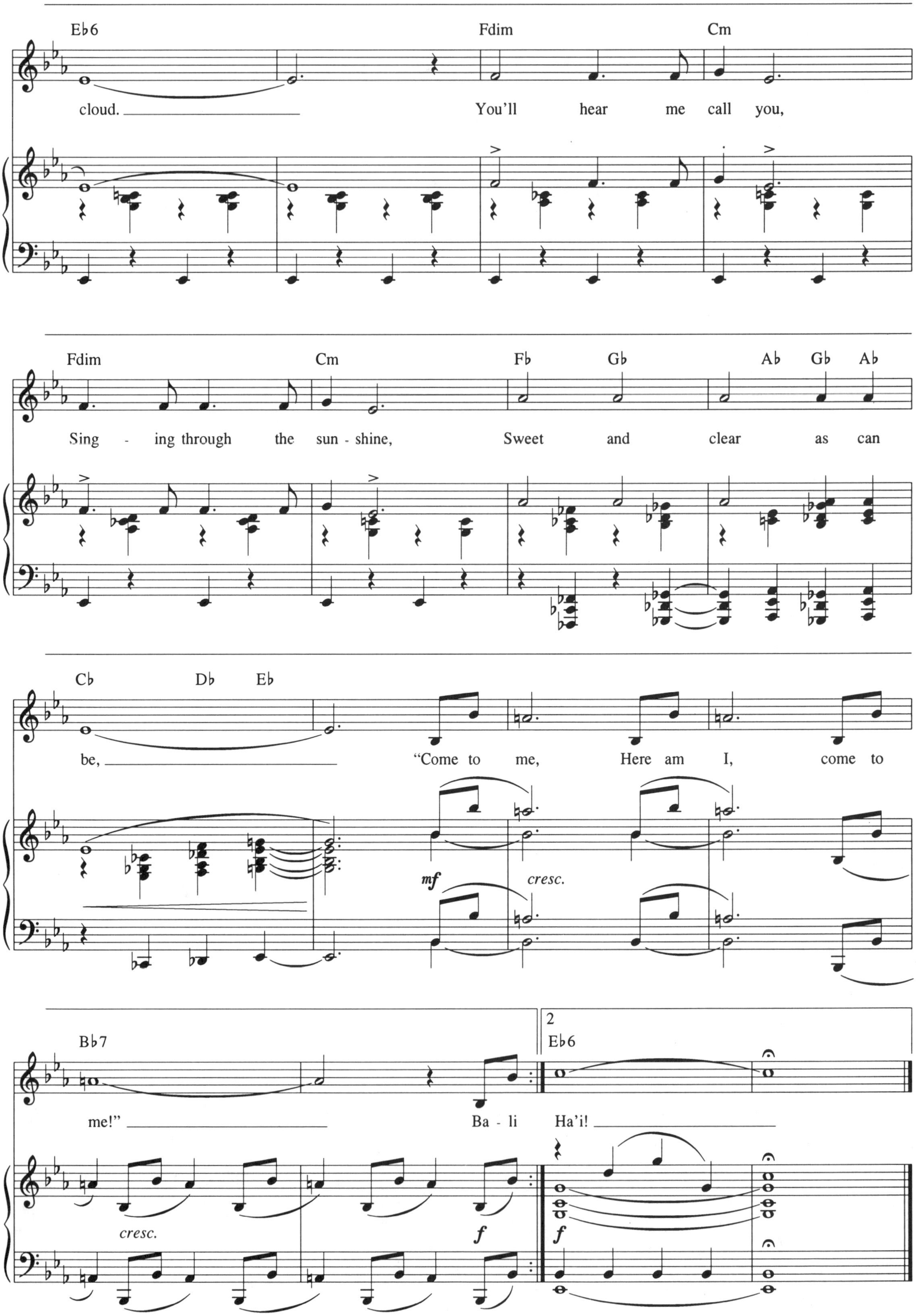
Eb6
Fdim
Cm
cloud. You'll hear me call you,
Fdim
Cm
Fb
Gb
Ab
Gb
Ab
Sing - ing through the sun - shine, Sweet and clear as can
Cb
Db
Eb
be, "Come to me, Here am I, come to
mf
cresc.
Bb7
2
Eb6
me!" Ba - li Ha'i!
cresc.
f
f

THE EARTH AND OTHER MINOR THINGS

GIGI

Words by ALAN JAY LERNER
Music by FREDERICK LOEWE

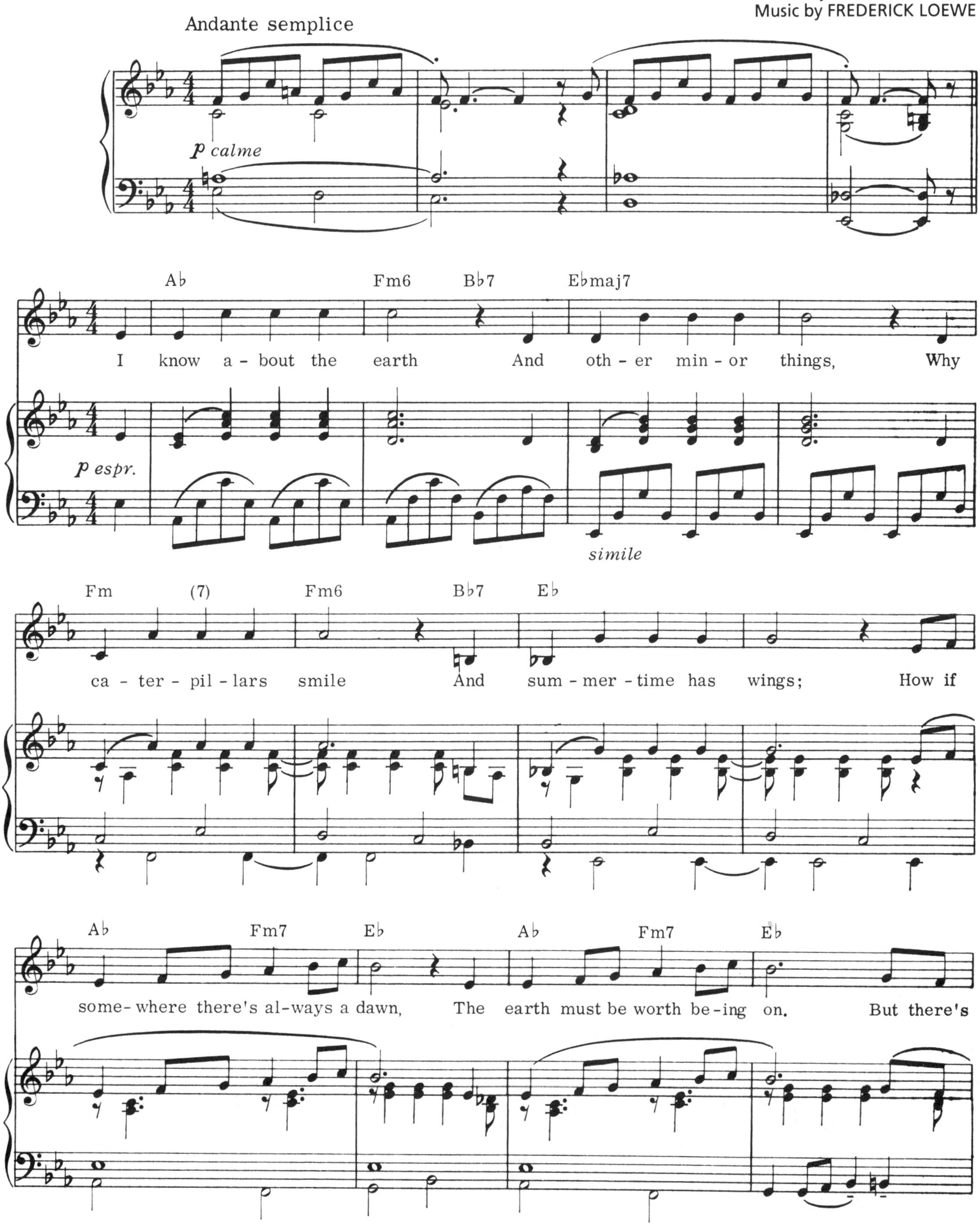
Andante semplice
p calme
Ab Fm6 Bb7 Ebmaj7
I know a - bout the earth And oth - er min - or things, Why
p espr.
simile
Fm (7) Fm6 Bb7 Eb
ca - ter - pil - lars smile And sum - mer - time has wings; How if
Ab Fm7 Eb Ab Fm7 Eb
some- where there's al - ways a dawn, The earth must be worth be - ing on. But there's

Cm Ab6 Eb Ab Eb/Bb Bb7
one thing that makes a con-tin - u-al rid-dle of it: Why, oh why I'm here in the mid-dle of it
colla voce
Eb Bb7/F Bb7 Ebdim Eb G7/B G7
all? I don't be-long where the crowds are. Why don't I go where the
espr.
Cm6 Cm Eb7 Ab Dm7 Ebmaj7
clouds are? I know a-bout the leaves That fall and then are gone; How
dolce
Fm7 Fm7/Bb Eb Ab
small a kite be-comes With no one hold-ing on; And I can't be a cloud in a

Eb Ab Eb G7 Cm Abm6
storm With no where to go to be warm; And as long as I can't find a
Eb/G Ab Eb/Bb Bb7 Eb
clue to the rid-dle of it, What am I to do in the mid - dle of it all?
colla voce
Bb7/F Bb7 Ebdim Eb G7/B Bdim Cm
I don't be-long where the crowds are. I don't be-long where the clouds are. Then
espr.
Fm7 Eb Fm Ab/Bb7 Eb
where do I be - long?
sost.
p

A COCK-EYED OPTIMIST

SOUTH PACIFIC

Lyrics by OSCAR HAMMERSTEIN II
Music by RICHARD RODGERS

cur - a - bly green! I have heard peo-ple rant and rave and
bel - low That we're done and we might as well be dead
But I'm on - ly a cock - eyed op - ti - mist And I
can't get it in - to my head. I hear the hu - man

poco rit
race Is fall - ing on its face And has - n't ver - y far to
poco rit
a tempo
go, But ev 'ry whip - poor - will Is sell - ing me a
3
a tempo
bill And tell - ing me it just ain't so. I could
say life is just a bowl of jel - lo, And ap - pear more in -
3

tel - li - gent and smart But I'm stuck (like a dope!) with a
thing called hope, And I can't get it out of my heart.
poco a poco cresc.
Not this heart.
(mf)

FALLING IN LOVE WITH LOVE

THE BOYS FROM SYRACUSE

Words by LORENZ HART
Music by RICHARD RODGERS

F7
dance,
And
mf
p
F7 sus.4
Cm7
F7
keep your hands out of ro - mance.
mf
Bb
G7(b9)
Love-ly witch - es, Let the
mp
Cm7
F7
Cm7
F7
Bb
stitch - es Keep your fin - gers un - der con - trol.

Gm
Cm
— Cut the thread, but leave ——— The
Cm7
F7
Bb
F7
whole heart whole. ———
mf
F7
Mer - ry maids can
p
F7
Cm7
G#dim7
F7
sew and sleep, Wives can on - ly sew and weep!
poco cresc.

Refrain
(Tempo moderato di Valse)
B♭ B♭maj7 B♭6 B♭ F7sus.4
Fall - ing in love with love Is fall - ing for make be -
p-mf
F7 Cm7 F7 F7sus.4 F7 F7sus.4
lieve. Fall - ing in love with love Is
F7 B♭maj7 B♭6 B♭maj7 B♭6 B♭maj7
play - ing the fool; Car - ing too
B♭6 B♭maj7 B♭6 D7sus.4 D7 F6
much is such a ju - ve - nile fan - cy.

D7 Gdim7 Gm Cm C7
Learn-ing to trust is just For chil-dren in
cresc.
Cm7 F7 B♭ B♭maj7
school. I fell in love with
dim.
p
B♭6 B♭ F7sus.4 F7 Cm7 F7
love one night When the moon was full,
F7sus.4 F7 F7sus.4 F7 B♭maj7 B♭6
I was un - wise with eyes Un - a-ble to see.

Bbmaj7 Bb6 Bbmaj7 Bb6 Bbmaj7 Bb6
I fell in love with love, With love ever-
D7sus.4 D7 Gmaj7 G7 Cm Ddim7
lasting, But love fell
cresc.
1.
Cm7 F7 Bb F7
out with me.
f
2.
Bb Bb6
me.
mf
f

GETTING TO KNOW YOU

THE KING AND I

Lyrics by OSCAR HAMMERSTEIN II
Music by RICHARD RODGERS

G7 Gm7 C7 Cm7
boast.) And I've now be - come an ex - pert On the sub - ject I like
(spoken)
F7
Refrain (gracefully and not fast)
B♭
most, Get-ting to know you. Get-ting to know you,
mp tranquillo
Cm7 F7 Cm7 F7 Cm7 F7
get-ting to know all a - bout you Get-ting to like you,
Cm7 F7 B♭ B♭
get-ting to hope you like me Get-ting to know you,

Ebmaj7 Eb6 Eb+ Eb
Put-ting it my way, but nice - ly You are pre -
cresc.
Gm7 C7 Cm7
cise - ly My cup of tea!
mf
F7 Bb
Get-ting to know you, get-ting to feel free and
f p
Cm7 F7 Cm7 F7 Cm7 F7 Cm7 F7
eas - y When I am with you, get-ting to know what to

Bb7
Ebmaj7
Eb6
Cm7
F7
say. Have-n't you not - iced? Sud-den-ly I'm bright and
Bbmaj7
Bb7
Eb
Bb
Cm7
F7
breez - y Be - cause of all the beau-ti-ful and new
poco a poco cresc.
Bb
Gm7
C7
Gm7
C7
Cm7
F7
things I'm learn-ing a-bout you day by
1
2
Bb
Cm7
F7
Bb
Eb
Bb
day. Get-ting to day.
f
p
mf

I ENJOY BEING A GIRL

FLOWER DRUM SONG

Lyrics by OSCAR HAMMERSTEIN II
Music by RICHARD RODGERS

Fmaj.7
swerv - y. I a - dore be - ing dressed in some - thing
G7
fril - ly When my date comes to get me at my place. Out I
B♭m6
go with my Joe or John or Bill - y, Like a
F F6 Fmaj.7 F C7 B♭ E♭m C7
fil - ly who is read - y for the race!

Refrain (brightly)
F6
When I have a brand new hair - do With my
mf
C7
eye - lash - es all in curl, I
F
D7
Gm
B♭m
float as the clouds on air do, I en -
F
C7
F6
F
joy be - ing a girl! When

F6
C7
men say I'm cute and fun - ny — And my teeth are - n't
F
D7
teeth but pearl, — I just lap it up like
Gm
B♭m
F
C7
F6
hon - ey — I en - joy be - ing a girl! —
F
B♭m
Fm
— I flip when a fel - low sends me flow - ers, — I
mf

B♭m
Fm
Fm7
Fm6
Fm
D♭
drool o - ver dress - es made of lace, I talk on the
A♭
A♭maj.7
A♭6
A♭
G7
tel - e - phone for ho - urs With a pound and a half of cream up - on my
C
B♭
C9
F6
face! I'm strict - ly a fe - male fe - male
C7
And my fu - ture I hope will be In the

F
D7
Gm
G9
F
home of a brave and free male Who'll en - joy be -
f
F6
Gm
B♭m
F
F7
F6
- ing a guy hav - ing a girl
C7(6)
1. F
D7(♭5)
like me.
f
Ped.
C7
2. F
When me.
f
sf
Ped.

I LOVE PARIS

CAN-CAN

Words and Music by
COLE PORTER

Moderato
mf
Tranquillo
C
F6
Ev - 'ry time I look down on this time - less town, wheth - er
p
G7
C
C6
Cmaj.7
C
blue or grey be her skies, Wheth - er
3
3
Gm6
A
A7
D7
loud be her cheers, or wheth-er soft be her tears, more and
mf

Fm6
G7(6)
F
G7(6)
G7
C
C dim.
G7(♭9)
more do I re - al - ize
poco rit.
Cm
Refrain (slow fox-trot tempo)
Cm
I love Par - is in the spring - time,
p legato
Cm
I love Par - is in the
G7
G7
fall,
I love

G7
Par - is in the win - ter, when it driz - zles,
Fm G7 Cm
I love Par - is in the sum - mer, when it siz - zles,
C
Sostenuto (jubilantly)
I love Par - is ev - 'ry mo - ment,
f
C Cdim.
ev - 'ry mo - ment of the

G7
Dm7
G7
F
year,
I
love
Par - is,
C
why, oh why do
F
C
I love Par - is?
1.
G7
C
Cdim.
G7
Be-cause my love is near.
p
rit.
a tempo
mf
2.
G7
A7(sus)
A7
Be-cause my love
p cresc.
Dm7
G7(sus)
C
Be-cause my love is near.
f
ff
Ped.
*

IF I RULED THE WORLD

PICKWICK

Words by LESLIE BRICUSSE
Music by CYRIL ORNADEL

Eb
Eb dim
1. Fm7
Bb7
sing of the joy ev-'ry morn-ing would bring. 2. If
word we would treas-ure each day that oc-
2. Fm7
G7
Cmaj.7
C6
Dm7
G7
curred. My world would be a beau-ti-ful place Where we would
mp
Cmaj.7
C6
Fm7
Bb7
Ebmaj.7
Eb6
weave such won-der-ful dreams. My world would wear a
Fm7
Bb7
G7
Cm
Eb6
Am7
smile on its face Like the man in the moon has when the moon

Fm7 Bb7 Eb Eb6 Ebmaj.7 Eb7
beams. If I ruled the world ev-'ry man would say the
mf
Dm7 G7
world was his friend, There'd be hap-pi-ness that
Cm F7
no man could end, No, my friend, not if
Eb Bbm6 C7b9 C7 Fm7
I ruled the world. Ev-'ry head would be

Bb7 Eb Bbm6
held up high, There'd be sun - shine in ev - 'ry - one's
C7b9 C7 Fm7 Bb9
sky If the day ev - er dawned when
Fm7 Bb9 Eb Abm6
I ruled the world.
Eb B♮7 Fm7 Bb7b5 Eb

IN MY OWN LITTLE CORNER

CINDERELLA

Lyrics by OSCAR HAMMERSTEIN II
Music by RICHARD RODGERS

Refrain (with tender expression)
C7 F Eb Eb6 Eb
In my own lit - tle cor - ner, in my own lit - tle chair, I can
mp
C7 F C7 F
be what - ev - er I want to be. On the wing of my
Eb Eb6 Eb C7
fan - cy I can fly an - y - where And the world will
F D
o - pen its arms to me. I'm a young Nor - we - gian
legato

A7(sus.) A7 F#m D Bm F#7
prin-cess or a milk - maid, I'm the great-est pri - ma don - na in Mi-
Bm D+ D Em7 A7
lan. I'm an heir-ess who has al-ways had her
D A E7
silk made By her own flock of silk-worms in Ja -
A Gm7 C7 F
pan. I'm a girl men go mad for, love's a
mp

E♭ F♭6 E♭ C7
game I can play with a cool and con-fi-dent kind of
F7 B♭ B♭m
air, Just as long as I stay in my own lit-tle
cresc.
mf
F B♭ F B♭ F Gm C7
cor - ner, All a - lone in my own lit - tle
1. F Gm7 C7
2. F
chair. In my chair.
mf
mf

IT MIGHT AS WELL BE SPRING

STATE FAIR

Lyrics by OSCAR HAMMERSTEIN II
Music by RICHARD RODGERS

Refrain
(gracefully)
dope.
I'm as rest - less as a wil - low in a
p
wind - storm, I'm as jump - y as a pup - pet on a string.
I'd say that I had spring -
fe - ver, But I know it is - n't spring.
I am star - ry eyed and vague - ly dis - con -
tent - ed, Like a night - in - gale with - out a song to sing.
Oh,

why should I have spring fe - ver When it is - n't e - ven spring?
I keep wish-ing I were some-where else, Walk ing down a strange new street,
Hear - ing words that I have nev - er heard from a { man / girl } I've yet to meet. I'm as
cresc.
mf
p
bus - y as a spi - der spin-ning day - dreams, I'm as gid - dy as a ba - by on a

swing. I have - n't seen a cro - cus or a rose - bud, or a
rob - in on the wing, But I feel so gay in a mel - an - cho - ly way that it
might as well be spring. It might as well be
1. spring!
2. spring!
mf
mf

MARIA

Lyrics by OSCAR HAMMERSTEIN II
Music by RICHARD RODGERS

Allegretto con moto

B♭/A Bm7 C7 F7 Cm7 F7
ri - a's not an as - set to the ab - bey. She's
f p
B♭ E♭/F B♭ F/A F9 E♭/B♭ B♭ B♭6 B♭ F9/A F7
al - ways late for chap - el But her pen - i - tence is real. She's
B♭ E♭/F B♭ F/A F9 E♭/B♭ B♭ B♭6 B♭ F9/A F7 D7/A
al - ways late for ev - 'ry - thing ex - cept for ev - 'ry meal. I
Gm Gm7/F Gm6/E E♭7 B♭/D E♭/D♭ Cm7
hate to have to say it but I ver - y firm - ly feel Ma -

B♭/F
Gm7
Cm6/E♭
D
Cm(add9)/E♭
D7
ri - a's not an as - set to the ab - bey. I'd
f
mp
Gm7
C9
F
Gm7
C7
like to say a word in her be - half. Ma - ri - a makes me
F
laugh!
Refrain (Moderately)
B♭
How do you solve a prob - lem like Ma -
p
F7
B♭
F
ri - a? How do you catch a cloud and pin it down?
mf

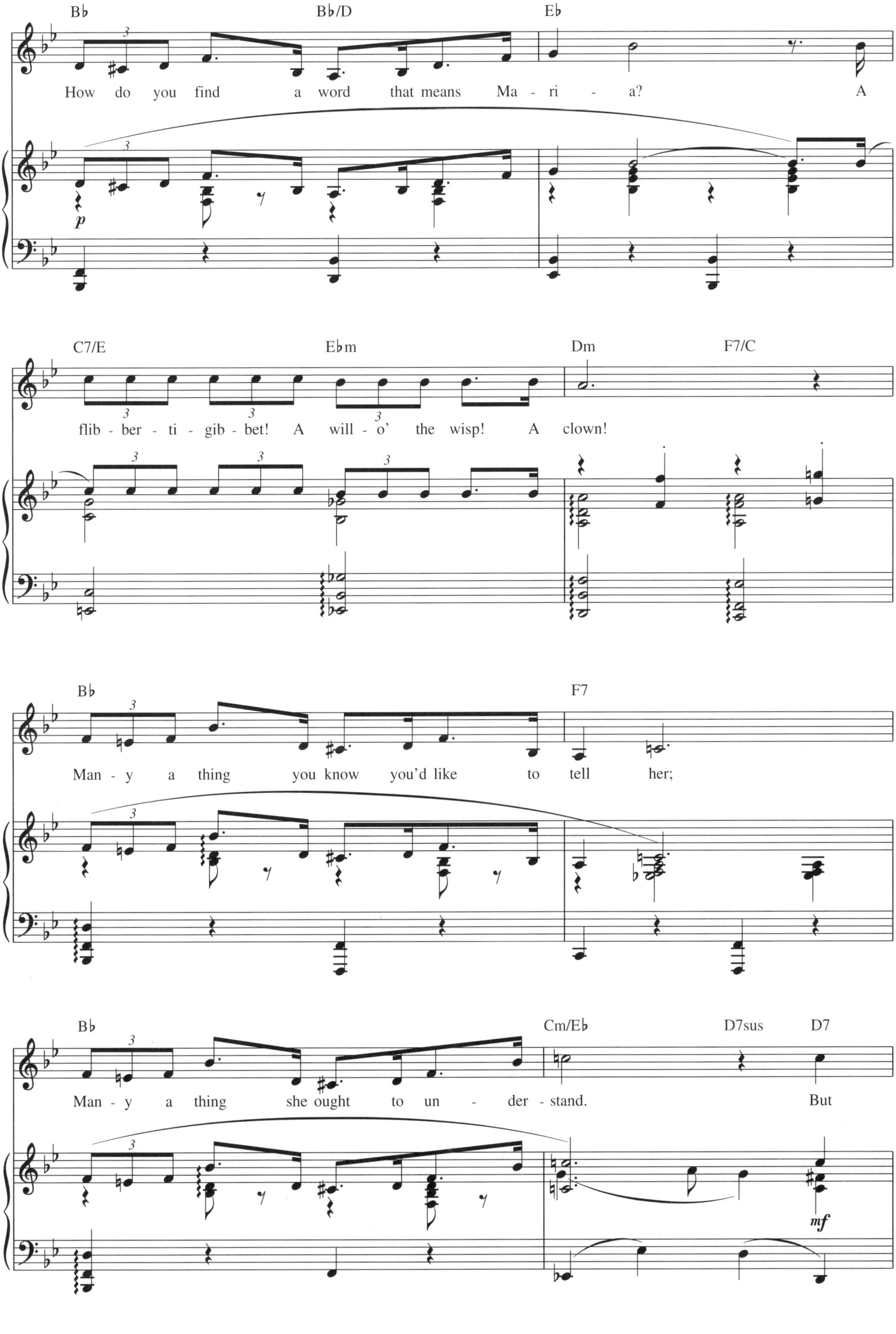

B♭ B♭/D E♭
How do you find a word that means Ma - ri - a? A
C7/E E♭m Dm F7/C
flib - ber - ti - gib - bet! A will - o' the wisp! A clown!
B♭ F7
Man - y a thing you know you'd like to tell her;
B♭ Cm/E♭ D7sus D7
Man - y a thing she ought to un - der - stand. But

B♭m/D♭
B♭m/F
F7/A
F7
how do you make her stay and lis - ten to all you say?
B♭m
F7
How do you keep a wave up - on the sand? Oh,
B♭
E♭
Cm7
B♭/F
B♭dim7/F
how do you solve a prob - lem like Ma - ri - a? How do you hold a
cresc.
f
Cm7
Cm7/F
F7
B♭
moon - beam in your hand?
espressivo

ON MY OWN

LES MISÉRABLES

Music by CLAUDE-MICHEL SCHÖNBERG
Lyrics by ALAIN BOUBLIL, HERBERT KRETZMER, JOHN CAIRD, TREVOR NUNN and JEAN-MARC NATEL

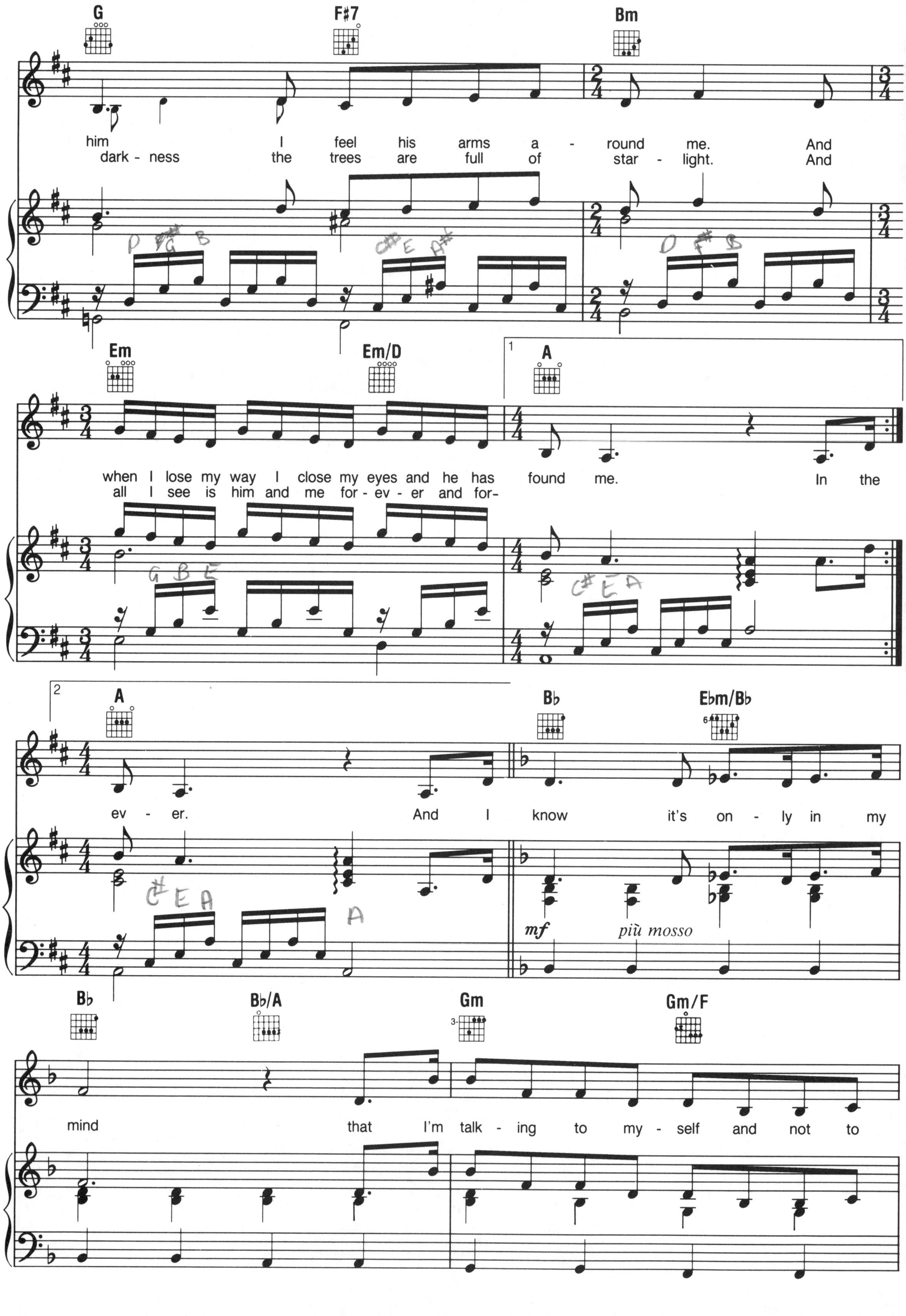
G
F♯7
Bm
him I feel his arms a - round me. And
dark - ness the trees are full of star - light. And
Em
Em/D
1
A
when I lose my way I close my eyes and he has found me. In the
all I see is him and me for - ev - er and for-
2
A
B♭
E♭m/B♭
ev - er. And I know it's on - ly in my
mf
più mosso
B♭
B♭/A
Gm
Gm/F
mind that I'm talk - ing to my - self and not to

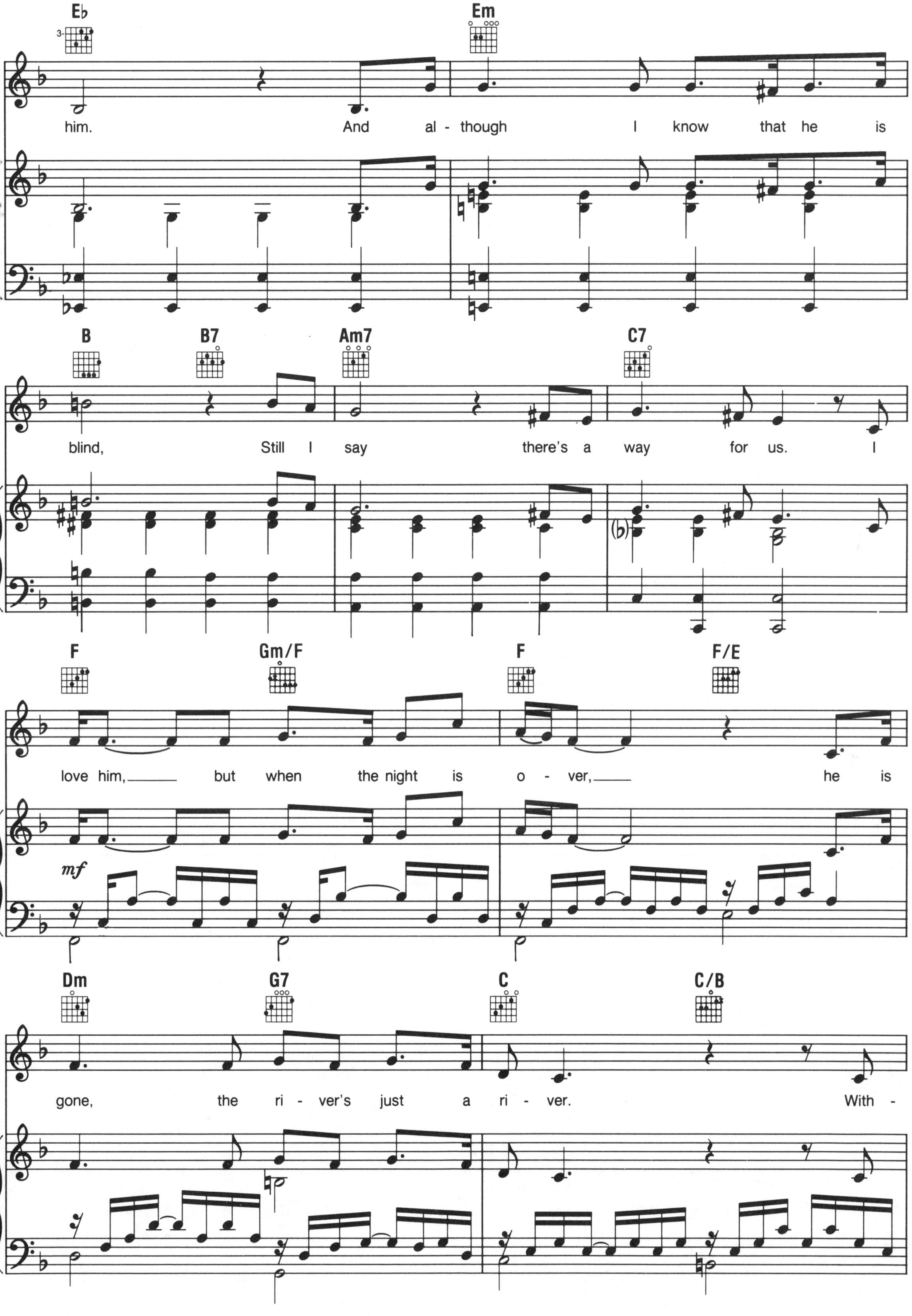
Eb
Em
him. And al - though I know that he is
B
B7
Am7
C7
blind, Still I say there's a way for us. I
F
Gm/F
F
F/E
love him, but when the night is o - ver, he is
mf
Dm
G7
C
C/B
gone, the ri - ver's just a ri - ver. With -

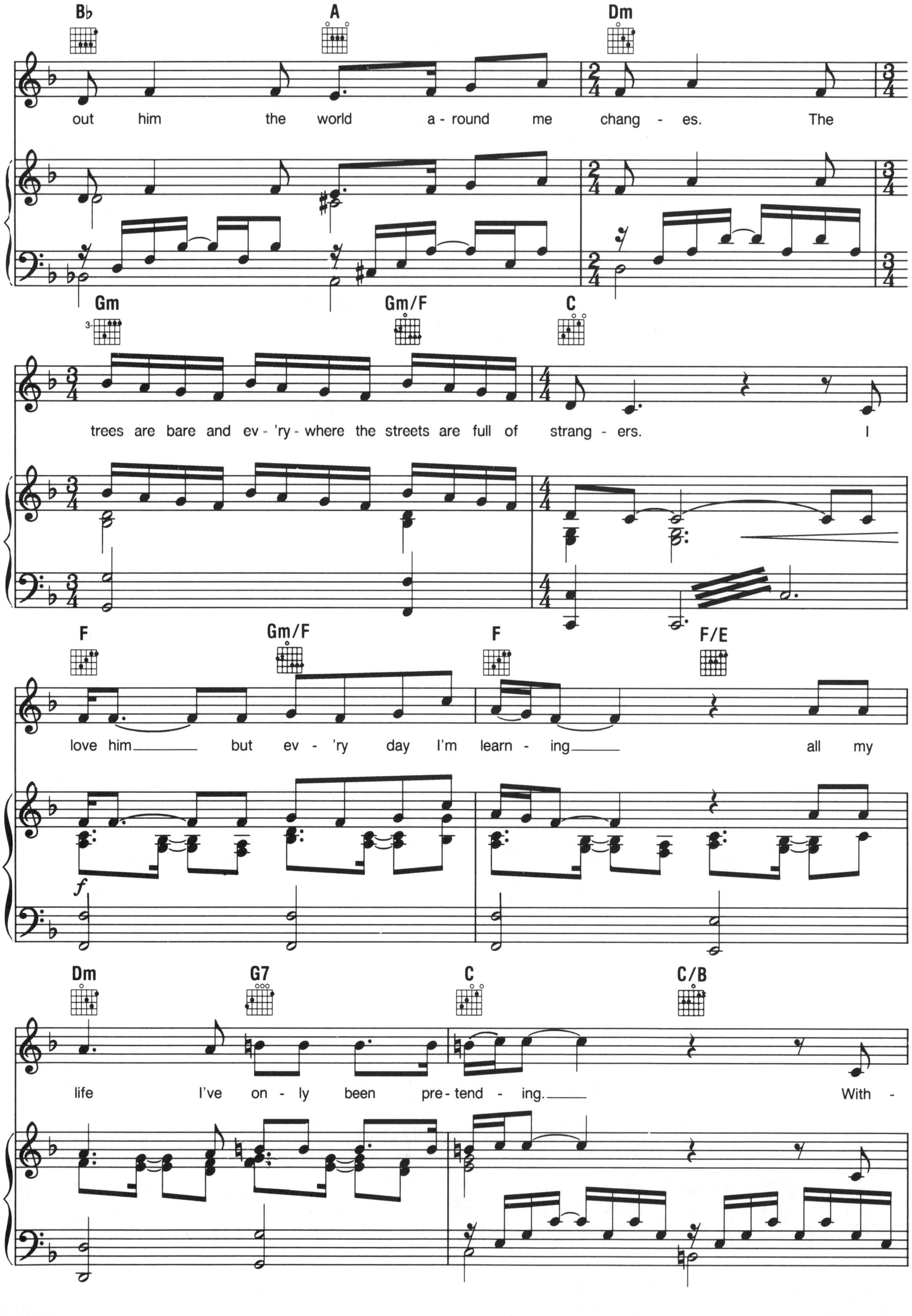
B♭ A Dm
out him the world a - round me chang - es. The
Gm Gm/F C
trees are bare and ev - 'ry - where the streets are full of strang - ers. I
F Gm/F F F/E
love him but ev - 'ry day I'm learn - ing all my
Dm G7 C C/B
life I've on - ly been pre - tend - ing. With -

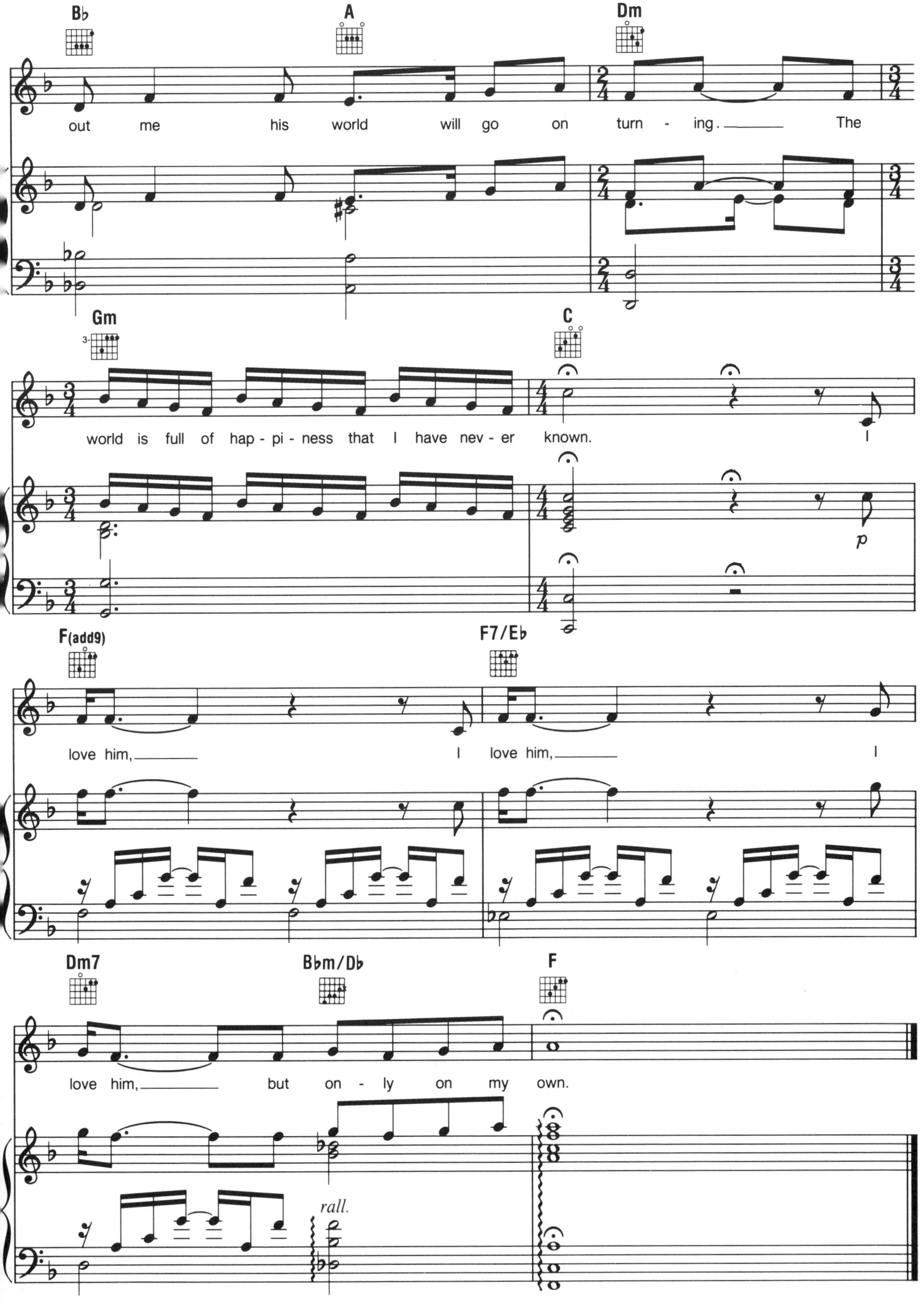
B♭
A
Dm
out me his world will go on turn - ing. The
Gm
C
world is full of hap - pi - ness that I have nev - er known. I
p
F(add9)
F7/E♭
love him, I love him, I
Dm7
B♭m/D♭
F
love him, but on - ly on my own.
rall.

MY FAVORITE THINGS

THE SOUND OF MUSIC

Lyrics by OSCAR HAMMERSTEIN II
Music by RICHARD RODGERS

Em
Cream col - ored pon - ies and crisp ap - ple
mf
mp
Cmaj.7
strud - els, Door-bells and sleigh - bells and schnitz - el with noo - dles,
Am7 D7 G C G
Wild geese that fly with the moon on their wings, These are a
C Am6 B7 E
few of my fa - vor - ite things.
f

E
A
Girls in white dress - es with blue sat - in sash - es, Snow-flakes that
mf
Am7
D7
stay on my nose and eye - lash - es, Sil - ver white win - ters that
G
C
G
C
Am6
B7
melt in - to springs, These are a few of my fa - vor - ite things.
Em
Am6
B7
When the dog bites, When the bee stings,
mf

Em
C
When I'm feel - ing sad,
I
C
A7
sim - ply re - mem - ber my fa - vor - ite things and
G C G
C G
D7(b9)
D7
G
then I don't feel so bad.
cresc.
f
C
G
D7
G
sf

MY FUNNY VALENTINE

BABES IN ARMS

Words by LORENZ HART
Music by RICHARD RODGERS

Cm Fm G
va - cant brow and thy tous - led hair con - ceal thy good in - tent. Thou
Cm B♭7 E♭ G G7+
no - ble, up - right, truth - ful, sin - cere and slight - ly dop - ey gent, you're
Refrain (slowly, with much expression)
Cm Cm(B♮) Cm7
My fun - ny Val - en - tine, Sweet com - ic
Cm6 A♭ Fm7
Val - en - tine, You make me smile with my

Fm6 G7 Fm G7 Cm G7
heart. Your looks are laugh - a - ble,
Cm7 Cm6 Ab Fm7
Un - pho - to - graph - a - ble, Yet, you're my fav - 'rite work of
Abm Bb7 Eb Bb7(Eb) Bb7 Eb Bb7(Eb) Bb7
art. Is your fig - ure less than Greek; Is your
mf
Eb Bb7(Eb) Bb7 Eb Bb7(Eb) Bb7 Ebmaj7 G7+ G7 Cm
mouth a lit - tle weak, when you o - pen it to speak, Are you

Abmaj7 Ab6 Ab7 G7 Cm Cm(B♮)
smart? But don't change a hair for me,
p
Cm7 Cm6 Ab D7b5 G7
Not if you care for me, Stay lit - tle Val - en - tine,
poco a poco cresc.
Cm Eb7 Ab Abmaj7 Fm7 Bb7
stay! Each day is Val - en - tine's
f molto espr.
mf
1. Eb Ab7 G7 2. Eb
day. day.
mf
p 8va

PEOPLE
FUNNY GIRL

Words by BOB MERRILL
Music by JULE STYNE

Fmaj.7 F6 G Bbm6 Gdim F Fdim Gm7 C7
pride Hide all the need in - side, Act - ing more like chil - dren, than
E F7 Cm7 F9 Bb F7
chil - dren. Lov - ers are ver - y spec - ial
rall.
mp a tempo
Bb Cm7 F7 Eb Bbmaj.7 Fm7
peo - ple, They're the luck - i - est peo - ple in the world.
3
Bb9 Bb7+ Eb Ebm Bb Fm7
With one per - son, One ver - y spe - cial per - son, A feel - ing

E♭ F7 B♭ Gm6
deep in your soul Says: you were half, now you're whole. No more
B♭6 Gm7 Cm7 F7 B♭
hun-ger and thirst, But first, be a per-son who needs peo-ple.
mf molto espressivo
B♭7(♭) E♭ E♭m E♭ B♭ Cm7
Peo-ple who need peo-ple Are the luck-i-est peo-ple in the
f
1. B♭ Gm7 Cm7 F7
world.
2. B♭ Gm7 B♭6
world.
rall.
p

SIMPLE LITTLE THINGS
110 IN THE SHADE

Words by TOM JONES
Music by HARVEY SCHMIDT

Dm7 Fm6 G7 C
Sim-ple lit-tle dreams will do.
8va
G7 Cmaj.7 G7
Hon-ey, is my blue suit pressed? Hon-ey, kind-a
mp
Cmaj.7 C6 G7 Am9
scratch be-tween my shoul-der blades. Hon-ey, are the chil-dren all in bed?
mf
Am6 D7 Dm7 Fm6 G7 Cmaj.7 Am7
That's what he'll say; I'll say "my hus-band." Sim-ple lit-tle things,
rall.
a tempo

Dm7 G9(sus.4) Em7 Am9 Dm7 Ddim
All I want are sim-ple lit-tle things. All I need is
f with emotion
Am Em F♯m7 B7
some-one be-side me to have and to hold, Some-one to love me as
più espressivo
G9 E7 Am7 Dm7 Fm6 G7
we grow old-er. Sim-ple lit-tle things, Sim-ple lit-tle dreams will
f with intensity
mp
1.C 2.C
do. do.
8va
dim. e rall.
p

SOMETHING WONDERFUL

THE KING AND I

Lyrics by OSCAR HAMMERSTEIN II
Music by RICHARD RODGERS

Molto moderato
mf
(slowly and smoothly)
G
G+
G7
Em6
This is a man who thinks with his heart, His heart is not al - ways
p
G
G+
wise. This is a man who stum - bles and falls, But
G7
Em6
G
Eb7+
this is a man who tries. This is a man you'll for -

Em6(F#)
F#
give and for - give and help and pro - tect, as long — as you
G
Moderato
F#
C
G
F#
C
live.
mf
dim.
C
G
D+
Refrain (slowly with expression)
G
D+
C
He will not al - ways say What you would have him say,
p
G
C
Am7
D7
But, now and then, he'll say some - thing won - der - ful.

G D+ C G D+ C
The thoughtless things he'll do Will hurt and worry you
G C A7 D
Then, all at once, he'll do something wonderful. He
Gm Dm Gm A7 D
has a thousand dreams that won't come true. You
più espressivo
Gm Gm7 A7 D
know that he believes in them And that's enough for you.
cresc.
mf

G D+ C G D+ C G
You'll al-ways go a-long, De-fend him when he's wrong And tell him
p
C A7 D B7 Em
when he's strong, He is won-der-ful. He'll al-ways need your love
mf
G7 C D+ C G
And so he'll get your love A man who needs your love can be
dim.
p
C
won-der-ful.
1. G F♯ C
2. G
mf
dim.
pp

THE SONG IS YOU

MUSIC IN THE AIR

Lyrics by OSCAR HAMMERSTEIN II
Music by JEROME KERN

Cmaj.9(F) C G7 G9 Cmaj.7 C Cdim(B) Cdim
start, Then melt a - way. I hear mu-sic when I touch your
p dolce
Dm7 G7 G9 C C6 Gdim Gdim(A)
hand, A beau - ti - ful mel - o - dy from some en - chant - ed
G7 C Cmaj.7 A7+
land, Down deep in my heart, I hear it
Dm G9 C
say, Is this the day?

E Emaj.7 A Dm B7
I a - lone have heard this lone - ly strain,
mp molto cantabile
E maj.7 D♯7
I a - lone have heard this glad re - frain,
G♯m G♯m7 C♯9
Must it be For - ev - er in - side of me, Why can't I
F♯7(6) F♯7 B7(6) B7
let it go, Why can't I let you know, Why can't I
cresc. e rall.

C maj.7 C B B7(♭9) G7 G7(C) G9
let you know the song my heart would sing, That beau-ti-ful
mf a tempo
C C6 C9 F Fm6
rhap-so-dy of love and youth and spring, The mu-sic is
C C maj.7 A7+ Dm G9
sweet, The words are true, The song is
C
you.
p tranquillo
pp
Ped.

WHERE OR WHEN

BABES IN ARMS

Words by LORENZ HART
Music by RICHARD RODGERS

Cm7 F7 B♭7 E♭7 B♭7 E♭7 A♭ Fm7
lived be-fore All that you live to-day. Things you do come back to you,
A♭m6 Fm7 B♭7 E♭ Fm B♭7 poco rit.
As though they knew the way. Oh, the tricks your mind can play!
poco rit.
Refrain E♭ with tender expression a tempo E♭6 E♭maj.7
It seems we stood and talked like this be-fore. We
a tempo
p
Fm7
looked at each oth-er in the same way then, But I can't re-mem-ber where or

E♭maj.7 E♭6 A♭m6 B♭7 E♭ E♭6
when. The clothes you're wear - ing are the
E♭maj.7 Fm7
clothes you wore. The smile you are smil - ing you were smil - ing then,
E♭maj.7 E♭6 Fm6 G7
But I can't re-mem-ber where or when.
Cm Fm7 G7(sus.4) G7 F G7 Cm
Some things that hap-pen for the first time, Seem to be
mp

Fm7 F7 sus.4 F7 Fm7 Bb7 Eb
hap - pen - ing a - gain. And so it
p
Eb6 Ebmaj.7 Eb+ Fm
poco a poco
seems that we have met be - fore, and laughed be -
poco a poco
Gm Fm Gm Fm sus.4 Fm Gm Bb7
crescendo e più espressivo
fore, and loved be - fore, But who knows where or
crescendo e più espressivo
1. Eb Fm7 Ebmaj.7 Fm7 Bb7
2. Eb Abm Cb Eb
mf rit.
when! when!
mf
mf
rit
L.H.

A WONDERFUL GUY

SOUTH PACIFIC

Lyrics by OSCAR HAMMERSTEIN II
Music by RICHARD RODGERS

Bb7 Dm Gm6 Dm Gm6 Dm Gm7 Dm A7
hear from a per-son in pants.
mf
D D
Fear - less - ly I'll face them and
mp
F# G C Em
ar - gue their doubts a - way
Loud - ly I'll
A7 Dmaj.7 D
sing a - bout flow - ers and spring.
Flat -

F# G C Em
ly I'll stand on my lit-tle flat feet and say Love
A7 D G
is a grand and a beau-ti-ful thing. I'm
A9 G A9 D Dmaj.7 D Dmaj.7 G
not a-shamed to re-veal The world
Gm A7(6) A+ A7(6) A+ A7
fa-mous feel-ing I feel.
f
rit.

Refrain (bright Valse tempo)
D Dmaj.7 D6 D Em7
I'm as corn - y as Kan - sas in Au - gust, I'm as
sf mp
A7 Em7 A7 D6
nor - mal as blue - ber - ry pie, No more a smart lit - tle
Em7 A7 D Em A7
girl with no heart, I have found me a won - der - ful guy!
D Dmaj.7 D6 D Em7 A7
I am in a con - ven - tion - al dith - er With a con - ven - tion - al
sf mp

Em7 A7 D6 Em7 A7
star in my eye. And you will note there's a lump in my throat When I
D Cmaj.7 C6 Dm7 G7
speak of that won-der-ful guy! I'm as trite and as
Cmaj.7 C6 Dm7 G7 Cmaj.7 C6
gay as a dai-sy in May, A cli-chè com-ing true!
Em7 A7 D D6 F♯m7 B7
I'm bro-mid-ic and bright as a moon-hap-py night Pour-ing light on the

E9 A9 D Dmaj.7 D7 D6
dew! I'm as corn - y as Kan - sas in Au - gust,
f mf mp
Gm A7 E7 A7 D7
High as a flag on the Fourth of Ju - ly! If you'll ex - cuse an ex -
cresc.
G Em7 D A7 D D+
pres - sion I use, I'm in love, I'm in love, I'm in love, I'm in love, I'm in
f
G Em 1. D A7+ 2. D
love with a won - der - ful guy! guy!
sf

WHAT'S THE USE OF WOND'RIN'

CAROUSEL

Lyrics by OSCAR HAMMERSTEIN II
Music by RICHARD RODGERS

C Am Dm G9 C A7 D7 D7(5♭) A♭7
Com-mon sense may tell you, that the end-in' will be sad, And now's the time to break and run a - way. But
C Am F C Dm7 C A9
what's the use of won-d'rin' if the end - in' will be sad? He's your fel-ler and you love him —
D7 Dm7 G9 C F
There's noth-in' more to say. Some-thin' made him the
C9 Fmaj.7 F F♯dim Gm7 C7(sus.6) F
way that he is — Wheth - er he's false — or true And some-thin' gave him the
p
f
mp

C9 Fmaj.7 F B7 E9 A7+ D9 G9+5 C Am
things that are his_ One of those things is you. So, When he wants your kiss-es, You will
mf
p
Dm G9 C A7 D7 Ab7 C Am
give them to the lad, And an-y-where he leads you, you will walk And an-y time he needs you, you'll go
F C Dm7 C A9 D7 Dm7 G9
run-nin' there like mad! You're his girl and he's your fel - ler And all the rest is
1. C Am Dm G7(C) G7
"talk."
2. C Fmaj.7 C
"talk."
f
f
sf
Ped.
*